AMERICAN TRAVELER

COLORADO AND THE ROCKIES

GALLERY BOOKS

An Imprint of W. H. Smith Publishers Inc.

112 Madison Avenue

New York City 10016

This edition first published in U.S.
in 1990 by Gallery Books,
an imprint of W.H. Smith Publishers, Inc.
112 Madison Avenue, New York, New York 10016

ISBN 0-8317-8834-8

Printed and bound in Spain

For rights information about the photographs in
this book please contact:

The Image Bank
111 Fifth Avenue, New York, NY 10003

Producer: Solomon M. Skolnick
Author: Erin Hennessey
Design Concept: Lesley Ehlers
Designer: Ann-Louise Lipman
Editor: Terri L. Hardin
Production: Valerie Zars
Photo Researcher: Edward Douglas
Assistant Photo Researcher: Robert Hale
Editorial Assistant: Carol Raguso

*Aspen, winter playground of
the Colorado Rockies.* Opposite:
*Situated in Rocky Mountain
National Park, Long's Peak, the
park's highest at 14,256 feet,
overlooks trout-filled streams
and valley pastures.*

Above: *Separating the rivers that flow east from those that flow west, the great Continental Divide winds down through the Rockies.* Opposite: *Looking west, beyond the Divide, snow-capped mountains stretch as far as the eye can see.*

The state of Colorado has an amazing diversity of terrain. The Rocky Mountains blast through the middle of the state, dividing east from west. Peaks, plateaus, and plains are also present, not to mention canyons, sand dunes, and great rushing rivers. There are 104,247 square miles to explore and elevations ranging from 3,350 feet to more than 14,000 feet above sea level.

In addition to Colorado's great outdoors, there are thriving four-season resorts and sophisticated cities that are full of historic interest. Denver, for example, is home of the U.S. Mint, the Mile High Stadium, and the "unsinkable" Molly Brown house. But since the mountains are so prominent an attraction, it seems fitting to begin with them.

Top to bottom: *Wind and weather eroded granite rises to 12,000 feet on Trail Ridge near Long's Peak. In Rocky Mountain National Park climbers frequently take on the challenge of scaling Chasm Lake. The alpine tundra of the park seems cold and stark in comparison to the surrounding mountains. In reality, the tundra is home to a myriad of unusual wildlife, a source of great enjoyment by the park's many visitors.* Opposite: *Quaking aspen explode into rich autumn color on the shores of Bear Lake in Rocky Mountain National Park.*

The Rockies extend all the way from central Alaska to the southern United States. The Grand Teton range in Wyoming makes up part of the range. And even farther north, the Rockies cut through the Canadian provinces of British Columbia and Alberta, where glacier-fed lakes, like ice-blue Lake Louise in Banff National Park, are a common sight, as are lush forests and snow-capped peaks.

The Rockies form a segment of a great mountain divide—called the Continental Divide—that continues on through the rest of the Americas to the south. On the west side of the Rockies are the snowy ramparts of the Divide, forming a North American watershed that separates the rivers that flow in an easterly direction from those flowing west.

The younger (geologically speaking) the mountain range, the higher and more rugged it is, because the forces of erosion have had less time to wear it down. As a whole, the Rockies are considered a middle-aged mountain range, younger than the Appalachians in the East, but quite a bit older than its more westerly neighbor, the Cascade range.

In summer, spectacular displays of wildflowers dot the rocky mountain-side. There are 84 peaks which exceed 11,000 feet in the park.

A statue of a bronco buster raises images of Colorado's humble beginnings. Below: *Denver, the state capital since 1876, is now home to over 500,000 and has become a great manufacturing, distribution, and transportation center, as well as the energy capital of the west.* Opposite: *Downtown Denver.*

The Rockies, like most mountain ranges, affect the weather. The western slopes of the Rockies receive most of the moisture, since the air cools as it rises over these slopes, while the eastern slopes tend to be dryer. In summer, one of the most common occurrences is the afternoon thunderstorm. But there can be rapid weather changes, with balmy breezes following on the heels of a rainfall.

Inspired by the Mall in Washington, D.C., Denver's Civic Center offers tourists and locals alike the chance to stroll and enjoy its three-block stretch of lawns and gardens. Below: *Gateway to the city.*

The Rockies feature national parks and monuments. The Rocky Mountain National Park, one of the biggest and most picturesque of all the parks, is located in the northwestern part of Colorado. It has the highest paved highway in the United States; one can drive for 15 miles above timberline, reaching 12,000 feet in altitude. Below is a stunning view of alpine meadows, forests, waterfalls, and deep mountain lakes. One of the most popular stops is the town of Estes Park, which features skiing facilities, a dinner theater, galleries, and plenty of restaurants.

But it is really the surrounding wilderness that draws the crowds. Hiking trails abound, and 44 lakes and numerous streams make it a great place to fish.

In the northwest is one of Colorado's more unusual attractions: The Dinosaur National Monument, a national preserve covering 325 square miles and spilling over into Utah. On exhibit is one of the world's

top to bottom: The Denver Center for the Performing Arts. Because of its elevation above sea level, Denver is known as the Mile High City. This thirteenth step on the site of the capital building is exactly one mile above sea level. Nearby mountains actually peak at over twice this altitude. The Denver Technical Center.

Capital Building at night. The Classic Revival design is modeled after the U.S. Capital Building and took over a decade to complete. Opposite: *Christmas lights illuminate the curved façade of Denver's City and County Building, built in 1932.*

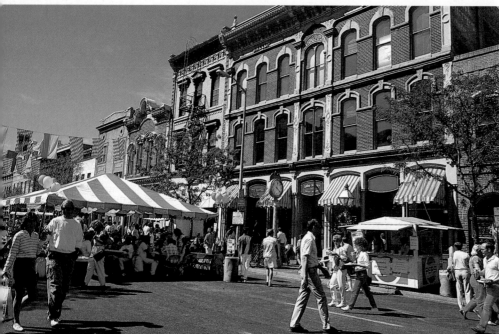

largest collections of fossilized dinosaur bones and more than 20 reconstructed skeletons—some dating back 100,000 years.

In Dinosaur National Monument are the sandstone cliffs that give this area of the state a distinctive beauty. The most dramatic rock formation is Steamboat Rock, rising 700 feet above the Yampa River below. This pinnacle consists of layers of sandstone that were once underwater. Besides looking spectacular, its broad sides reflect sound waves, which help to put the echo in nearby Echo Park.

Along the western side of the Colorado Rockies is legendary ski country. It is here that world-class resorts like Vail and Aspen are found.

Vail is located in the Gore Creek Valley, sandwiched between the Gore and Sawatch mountain ranges. Opened as a ski resort in the early 1960's, the site attracts skiers from around the world; its wide-mouth bowls offer lots of

Top to bottom: *This 42-room mansion was built in 1902 by Governor James B. Grant. The brick buildings in Larimer Square Historic District, built between 1870 and 1890, replaced the wooden structures which were destroyed by fire and floods in 1863 and 1864. The restored "House of Lions" was home to the "Unsinkable" Molly Brown, a celebrated survivor of the Titanic's disastrous maiden voyage.*

East of Larimer Square is the Tabor Center Shopping Mall. Below: *The conservatory at the Denver Botanic Gardens contains a tropical/sub-tropical forest.*

Above, left to right: *The Tivoli Brewery, built in the Second Empire style, now houses shops and restaurants. The Denve. branch of the U.S. Mint has been operating in its current building since 1906. One and one-half million dollars in coins are stamped out here daily. The Navarre, currently the home of the Museum of Western Art, was previously a casino and a co-educational college.* Below: *The Denver Technical Center.* Opposite: *The "1999" Building now towers above the Holy Ghost Church.*

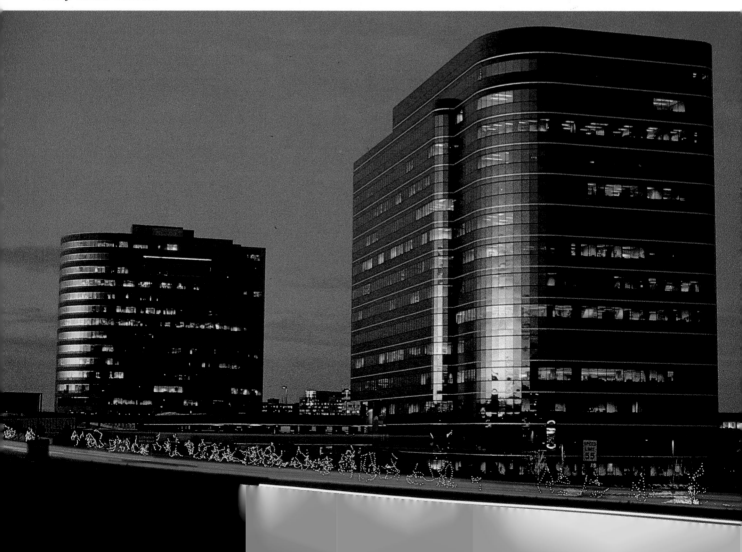

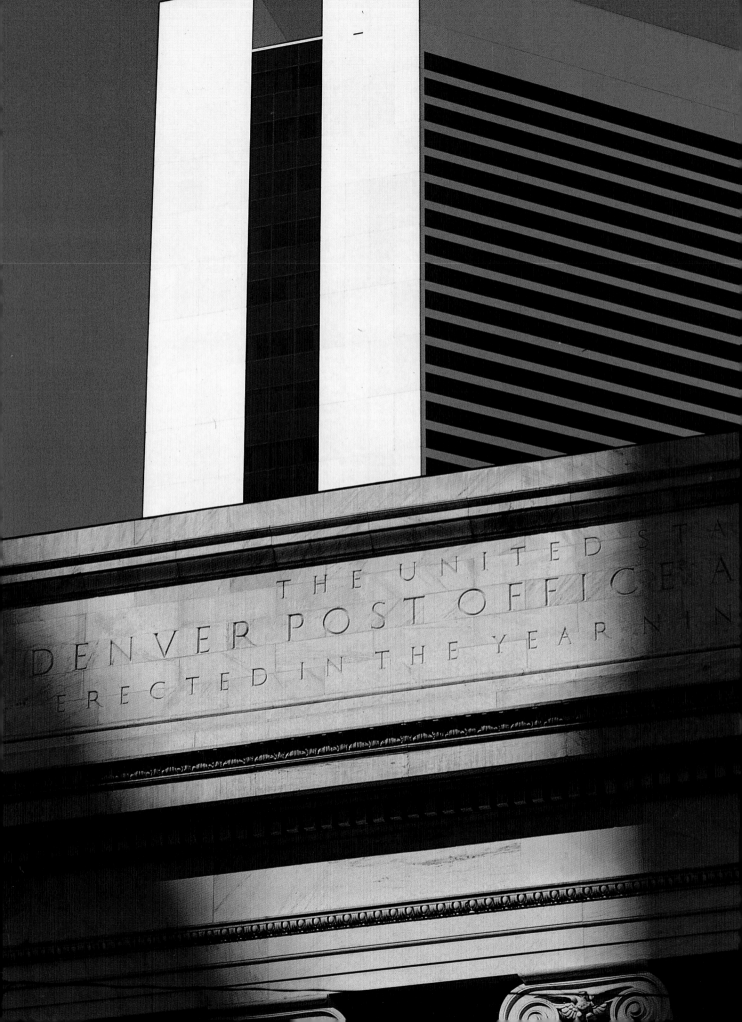

room and variety for those making their way down the slopes. Self-consciously comparing itself to villages in the Swiss Alps, the town of Vail is decked out to resemble a European mountain village, but with all the luxuries of a modern city.

The Gore Range, which can be seen in its full splendor from Vail, is one of the most rugged areas in the Colorado Rockies. The Gores receive quite a bit of rain, and the forests climb high. At lower altitudes, the terrain remains green and heavily forested, with rushing creeks fed by the melting snows.

The other range that cradles Vail is the Sawatch. These mountains run north and south for a distance of almost 100 miles. It is a high range, claiming 15 peaks that rise over 14,000 feet, and many more over 13,000 feet.

Although Vail is the largest single-mountain skiing complex in Colorado, Aspen is the more glamorous of the two. If celebrity-watching and the chic side of skiing is what one craves, then Aspen is the place to go.

Preceding page: The façade of the U.S. Post Office building. This page: Mile High Stadium, home of the Denver Broncos of the National Football League. The Broncos have developed a loyal following including fans like "The Barrel Man."

Aspen started out as a silver prospecting town, and the nearby mines made it a thriving community in the late 1800's. During that time, many Victorian-style buildings were erected, some of which still stand. Above the town sits Mt. Aspen with its modern gondolas. Large modern houses are also scattered among the hills.

The current town of Leadville (formerly Oro City) sits between Vail and Aspen. The mountains around Leadville have one of the highest mineral concentrations in the world. Gold was discovered there in 1860, but it played out after yielding $10 million in a little more than 10 years.

At a point when the town was on the verge of being abandoned, William Stevens and Alvinus Woods found nearly pure lead carbonate with silver in the abandoned gold mines. By 1878, the new rush was on, and the town was reborn as Leadville. Exhibits at Leadville's Heritage Museum and Gallery tell these and other interesting stories about the mining town's early days.

Preceding page: *This natural red sandstone amphitheater in Red Rocks Park near Denver seats 10,000 people. This page: Cadets at the U.S. Air Force Academy on graduation day. An F104A Starfighter on the grounds of the Academy in Colorado Springs.*

Preceding page: *U.S. Air Force Academy Chapel.* This page, left to right: *Colorado Springs: A display from Pro Rodeo Hall of Fame and Museum of the American Cowboy. Shopping on the refurbished streets of "Old Colorado Springs." Typical wares and implements on display in a recreated nineteenth century "ghost town."* Below: *Opened in 1918, the lavish Broadmoor Hotel was designed by the architects who created New York's Grand Central Station and the Biltmore Hotel.*

Heading farther south is one of Colorado's natural wonders: the Black Canyon. Narrower and deeper than any other canyon in the country, Black Canyon shoots 2,700 feet down and 1,100 feet across. Its dark granite walls have been carved by the Gunnison River and it is part of the Gunnison National Monument. Many consider this area to have the best fishing in the state, although parts of it are protected.

The San Juan Mountains greet those who continue south. The Continental Divide moves along the crest of these mountains, with the Rio Grande River cutting a great swathe through its hills. The geological character of this area is varied, with peaks of granite and mountains composed of sedimentary rock. Old mining towns are scattered throughout this region as well, and some mining still takes place.

Above: *Fossilized impressions of insects, fish, and birds that lived 35 million years ago and giant "petrified" sequoias are the spectacular attractions at the Florissant Fossil Beds National Monument.* Left and opposite: *Pikes Peak National Historic Landmark and Forest bear the name of Zebulon Pike whose 1806 expedition was unable to reach the top of the peak. Over 70 years later, traveling Pikes Peak on an established trail, Katherine Lee Bates was inspired to begin composing "America The Beautiful.*

This page and opposite: *The "Garden of the Gods" in Colorado Springs, a stone Eden created by sedimentary rock thrust up 65 million years ago.*

In the extreme southwest
[co]rner of Colorado is a region
[kn]own as The Four Corners,
[w]here Colorado, Utah,
[A]rizona, and New Mexico
[m]eet. It is the only place in
[th]e United States where four
[st]ates come together.

In the Colorado corner is
[M]esa Verde National Park,
[co]ntaining the ancient cliff
[d]wellings of the Anasazi
[In]dians. The tribe that built
[th]is community almost 1,400
[ye]ars ago has since dis-
[ap]peared; the site itself,
[w]hich includes a two-story
[ho]use and a 200-room palace,
[w]as discovered by William
[H]. Jackson in 1874.

In the south central
[re]gion of the Colorado
[Ro]ckies sits yet another
[un]usual sigh s and
[m]iles of gian nes.
[T]he Great S
[N]ational Mo
[7]55 square mi
[sh]ifting sand, wit
[du]nes—the highest t
[na]turally formed in thi
[co]untry—rising 800 feet
[ab]ove the desert floor.

[Pr]eceding page: *North of the "Four
[C]orners" where Colorado, Utah,
[A]rizona, and New Mexico meet are
[th]e rugged San Juan Mountains
[w]hich boast some of Colorado's
[hi]ghest peaks and most severe
[va]lleys.* This page, center and
[bo]ttom: *Great Sand Dunes National
[M]onument in the San Luis Valley
[ha]s dunes which rise up 700 feet
[fr]om the valley floor.*

The mood of this region changes. According to the time of day and the type of light falling on the sand, the dunes take on different colors, and shadows come and go.

Wind and heat, rising from the sands, creates an imbalance in the atmosphere that encourages thunderstorms. These storms are in turn accompanied by giant bolts of lightning, for which the area is famous.

The southeastern region of Colorado is where the plains meet the mountains. Much of its flat lands resemble Kansas, which lies directly to the east. The Arkansas River runs through here, flowing easterly until it finally joins the Mississippi.

The city of Pueblo is located on the banks of the Arkansas, near the east flank of the Rockies. Known as a trading fort in the mid-1800's, it later became known for its steel industry. The Pueblo Reservoir is the largest body of water in southern Colorado. It boasts a shoreline of more than 60 miles and offers good fishing, boating, and water sports.

Top to bottom: *Main Street in Telluride. On the heels of substantial strikes of silver and gold by J. B. Ingram, Telluride was founded in 1878. It "hosted" Butch Cassidy's first bank job. Molas Lake, surrounded by mountains, sits at 10,500 feet. The site of Mesa Verde National Monument was discovered in 1874. Built almost 1,400 years ago by the Anasazi, it is an architecturally advanced and beautiful stone city.*

With a clear view of the Rockies, the plains are home to most of Colorado's population. Heading north from Pueblo, is Colorado Springs, the state's second-largest city. Colorado Springs is a fast-growing area that has as much of a rodeo atmosphere as it does a high-tech corridor. It still carries with it a strong feel of the Old West, but as more people move in and new businesses open up, it is moving toward meeting the challenges of the next century. Colorado Springs also houses the U.S. Olympic Training Center, where superb facilities attract top athletes.

Nearby is the U.S. Air Force Academy. Jets are a common sight, as are the cadets who fly them. For those interested in aviation and military history, the grounds of the Academy are well worth a visit.

Another one of Colorado Spring's neighbors is Pike's Peak, which rises like a pyramid when backlit by the setting sun. Towering over the city at 14,110 feet, the Pike defeated Zebulon Pike, who failed to scale it in 1806.

This page top: *A mining building from the boom days in Rico.* Right: *A coal train on the Narrow Gauge Silverton Line which runs through the San Juan Mountains to Durango.*

Preceding pages, left: *The dramatic Black Canyon in the Gunnison National Monument, 2,700 feet down and 1,100 feet across, is the deepest and narrowest in the U.S.* Right: *Ciulanti Needle Overlook in the Rockies. Saddlehorn and the Bookcliffs (opposite) are two of the prominent formations in the Colorado National Monument near Grand Junction.*

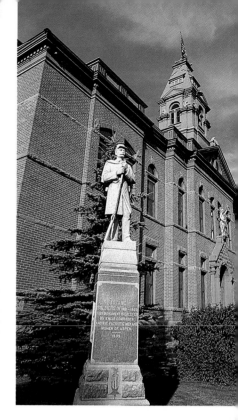

Preceding page: *Aspen, the Red Onion; Ski Gondola in one of Colorado's premier ski resorts. The Aspen police station.* Below: *A fairy-tale setting: winter snow settles on Aspen.*

Above: Ski jumping with Aspen and the Roaring Fork Valley laid out below. Below: The Lead King Mill in the River Valley provided power to miners in the 1890's. Overleaf: The Maroon Bells and the glacial lakes they feed lie west of Aspen in the Maroon Bells/Snowmass Wilderness.

The summit was reached by Major Stephen H. Long's party in 1820. Over 70 years later, a dirt road wound to the top, and reaching the peak could be accomplished in a buggy. It was on such a ride that Katherine Lee Bates was inspired to begin writing "America the Beautiful."

Since 1916, there has been an annual Fourth-of-July auto race up the side of its slopes on the zigzag road built by Stephen Penrose the year before.

Another natural spot that's worth a stop in this range is the Garden of the Gods. Covering over 1,350 acres, this "garden" consists of giant sandstone pillars and jagged spires. The bed of long-vanished seas, the Garden took shape some 70 million years ago. During this time, as new mountains were taking shape, its rocks were raised, tilted, and gnarled. Since then, the wind and water have sculpted the red sandstone cliffs into unusual shapes that capture the imagination.

Top to bottom: *The "Swiss" village in Vail, built in 1962, in the Gore Creek Valley. Vail served as the "western White House" during Gerald Ford's presidency. Leadville, situated at 10,000 feet, rewarded those brave or foolish enough to endure the harsh winters. One of the many abandoned mines in the Leadville area, relics of the final "bust" at the turn of the century.* Opposite: *A mogul field on the slopes of Vail, Colorado's largest single-mountain ski resort.*

Above: *Steamboat rock carved by the confluence of the Yampa and Green Rivers is 700 feet above the river that once covered it. Almost two dozen dinosaur skeletons were removed from this area (now Dinosaur National Monument) and are displayed at a nearby museum.* Opposite: *The Yampa River near the town of Steamboat.*

This page: *Crested Butte had a modest gold strike before it became fully established during a coal boom in the 1870's. The fine Carpenter Gothic buildings which were constructed during the 1870's and 1880's are now part of the Crested Butte National Historic District.*

Although the state's
dinosaur fossils sit on the
northwest side of the Colorado
Rockies, the eastern side of
the mountains can also
claim its share of venerable
discoveries. The Florrisant
Fossil Beds National
Monument, near Pike's Peak,
is an ancient riverbed.
Thousands of fossils dating
back 35 million years have
been found between its layers
of shale, including those of a
mastodon (discovered in the
nineteenth century).

Traveling north, one
reaches capital city Denver,
which replaced Golden, the
territorial capital, when
Colorado gained its state-
hood in 1876. Known as the
"Mile High City" (because it
sits a mile above sea level),
as well as the "Queen City of
the Plains". To its
west are the Rockies, rising
high and white behind the
city's tallest skyscrapers.

*Top to bottom: Georgetown was
an important silver center until the
silver crash of 1893. Maxwell House
is one of 200 Victorian homes which
remain. The University of Colorado
at Boulder opened in 1877. In 1859
gold-seekers built cabins and an
irrigation system along what is now
the Pearl Street Historic Commercial
District. The founders named their
town for the huge boulders in the
nearby Flat Iron Range.*

View from Arapajo to Basin as seen from Keystone. Below: Breckenridge, in the Ten Mile Range, was a vital gold mining town in the 1860's and silver center through WW II. Listed as a "ghost town" in the 1950's, its renaissance began with the building of a ski resort in the early 1960's. Opposite: These petroglyphs in Horseshoe Canyon were created between 700–1,100 years ago.

Preceding page and below: *Bryce Canyon National Park's walls form natural amphitheaters. Spires and pinnacles exhibit dramatic shifts in color as the light and weather change.* Below: *Horseshoe Canyon, in Canyonlands National Park. Rocks, spires, and mesas in the park rise as high as 7,800 feet.*

The city's architecture is a grand mix, from stately stone structures to modern glass towers. Denver's Civic Center was modeled after the Capitol Mall in Washington, D.C. Denver's own Capitol Building, surrounded by handsomely landscaped lawns and gardens, is capped with a gold dome.

There are over 20 historic districts in Denver, including Larimer Square, which was named after the city's founder, William Larimer, and had been Denver's original business district. The restored brick buildings in this district date from 1870-1890; these had replaced wooden structures that either burned down in the fire of 1863 or were destroyed in the flood of 1864.

Denver still has its share of grand historical buildings, including the Colorado Governor's Mansion, the Tabor Grand Opera House, and a number of beautiful Victorian-style homes. Many of these are located in the Ninth Street Historical Park. The Molly Brown House, home of that "unsinkable" survivor of the *Titanic,* is also in Denver.

This page: *Grand Teton National Park encompasses, within its borders, nearly the entire Teton Range. South, Middle, and Grand Teton (at 13,770 feet, the tallest peak in the range) as seen across Jenny Lake.*

Preceding page: *The Lower Falls of the Yellowstone River cascade over 300 feet into the canyon.* This page: *Crisp cold air and bubbling hot water make winter in Yellowstone National Park more spectacular than any other season. Over half of the world's geysers can be found in this park.* Bottom: *Hidden Lake in Glacier National Park.*

One of Colorado's smaller jewels is the city of Boulder, about 30 miles north of Denver. The University of Colorado's main campus is there, giving the town a young, academic atmosphere. Leafy streets with low buildings characterize much of the town.

One may seek the urban centers of Denver and Boulder, or the recreational centers of Vail and Aspen; or visit the majestic Rocky Mountains, and nearby lakes and parks. Whatever the destination, Colorado is a wonderful place with lively inhabitants—expansive, welcoming, and full of surprises.

St. Mary Lake and Wild Goose Island on the eastern slope of Logan Pass in Glacier National Park.

A portion of the 125-mile Columbia Ice Fields on Mt. Andromeda in the Canadian Rockies. Below: Mt. Robson at the edge of Jasper National Park in Alberta rises to almost 13,000 feet. Opposite: Lake Louise is fed by Victoria Glacier in the distance. Following pages: Helmut Falls in Kootenay National Park in British Columbia. Roger's Pass in the Canadian Rockies.

Index of Photography

All photographs courtesy of The Image Bank, except where indicated.*

Page Number	Photographer	Page Number	Photographer
Title Page	Grafton Marshall Smith	31 Bottom	Grant V. Faint
3	Jack Olson*	32 Top	Dann Coffey
4 Top	Sonja Bullaty	32 Center	John Lewis Stage
5	Jack Olson*	32 Bottom	L. Sedwin/Stockphotos, Inc.*
6 Top	Kent and Donna Dannen*	33 Top	Ed Cooper*
6 Center	David Hiser	33 Bottom	Sobel/Klonsky
6 Bottom	Sonja Bullaty	34	Jack Olson*
7	Kent and Donna Dannen*	35	George Obremski
8-9	Lionel Isy-Schwart	36 Top	Mark E. Gibson*
10 Top	Jake Rajs	37	John Kelly
10 Bottom	Andy Caulfield	38 Top left	Norm Clasen
11	Jake Rajs	38 Top Center	Alan Becker
12 Top	Jack Olson*	38 Top Right	Mark E. Gibson*
12 Bottom	Alan Becker	38 Bottom	David Brownell
13 Top	Larry Dale Gordon	39 Top	David Brownell
13 Center	Nick Nicholson	39 Bottom	Kent and Donna Dannen*
13 Bottom	Grafton Marshall Smith	40-41	David Brownell
14	Jack Olson*	42 Top	Jack Olson*
15 (2)	Jack Olson*	42 Center	Michael Melford
16 (3)	Jack Olson*	42 Bottom	George Obremski
17 Top	Andy Caulfield	43	Peter Miller
17 Bottom	Jack Olson*	44	Larry Pierce/Stockphotos, Inc.*
18 Top Left	Andy Caulfield	45	David Hiser
18 Top Center	Michael Kimak	46 Top	Dann Coffey
18 Top Right	Jake Rajs	46 Bottom	Grafton Marshall Smith
18 Bottom	Dann Coffey	47 (3)	Jack Olson*
19	Andy Caulfield	48 Top	Pete Turner
20	Andy Caulfield	48 Bottom	Jack Olson*
21 (2)	Jack Olson*	49	David Hiser
22	Jack Olson*	50 Top	Jeff Hunter
23 Top	Larry Pierce/Stockphotos, Inc.*	50 Bottom	Michael R. Schneps
23 Bottom	Dave Sternik/Stockphotos, Inc.*	51	Marc Romanelli
24	Mark E. Gibson*	52-53	Morton Beebe
25 (3)	Mark E. Gibson*	54	Michael R. Schneps
25 Bottom	Tim Beiber	55 Top	Robin Lehman
26 Top	Jack Olson*	55 Bottom	Steve Satushek
26 Bottom	Charles A. Nesser/Stockphotos, Inc.*	56-57	William A. Logan
27	Jack Olson*	58 Top	Richard & Mary Magruder
28 Top	John Kane/Stockphotos, Inc.*	58 Bottom	Pat O'Hara*
28 Bottom	Butch Powell/Stockphotos, Inc.*	59	Grant V. Faint
29	Alvis Upitis	60	Robert Villani*
30	John Kelly	61	Grant V. Faint
31 Top	Hans Wendler	62-63	Steve Satushek
31 Center	David Hiser		

Preceding pages: *Mt. Assinboine surrounded by Cerulean Lakes in British Columbia.*